THE HAIGHT-ASHBURY

The Haight-
1967, the
also about
Since the
farmers, vac
psychedelic rock stars. An early ad for real estate in the Haight read, ***"Once you see this beautiful land, you'll never want to live anywhere else."*** Since its beginning as a neighborhood, the Haight has been known as a place where people think for themselves.

Encircled by Golden Gate Park and its Panhandle, Buena Vista Park, Mt. Sutro and Tank Hill, the Haight's unique geography and the surviving mélange of Victorian and Edwardian architecture made it the ideal locale for an explosion in the '60s of a ***"nonconformist movement transforming Haight Street with reverberations felt around the world,"*** to paraphrase author K. Powell Cohen.

Faced with the horrors of the war in Vietnam, but buoyed by a new idealism of peace and love (not to mention newly available LSD, plentiful marijuana and birth control pills), the 60s generation found a conducive atmosphere in the Haight, where a new consciousness was born.

That attitude is still in the air, which is why shaggy-looking wanderers, backpacking students, tourists, and people of all races and walks of life can be seen on Haight Street. It can be a bit overwhelming sometimes, but neighbors all live in relative peace and many know each other. There's a **creative energy,** a raw edge, and a sense of being part of a **very special community** that includes those who are just visiting.

Read on to find out where it all took place, what happened to the Flower Children (a few are still here!), and why people come from all over the world to experience the **Haight-Ashbury Phenomenon.**

Dennis L. Maness

Contents

THE HAIGHT BEFORE 1906

The Extraordinary San Francisco Gold Rush

Early in 1848, James Marshall was working at John Sutter's lumber mill in the Sierra foothills. One day, he announced to Sutter that **he'd found gold** in the mill's watery tailrace! As the news spread, most people left the village of Yerba Buena for the gold fields. Later, that village became the booming City of San Francisco, where gold seekers from around the world made a life together.

Golden Gate Park: An Amazing Feat

In 1869, Mayor McCoppin approved a proposal for a city park to be built in The Outside Lands, and the City's first Parks Commission was appointed by Governor Henry **Haight.** To stabilize the dunes, first grasses, then trees were planted, primarily blue gum eucalyptus, Monterey pine, and Monterey cypress. Railroad magnates Crocker, Hopkins, Huntington, and Stanford wanted to build a racetrack instead of a park, but the park's popularity won out. As developers had anticipated, the park spurred the western expansion of the City.

Golden Gate Park, 1892

The Haight-Ashbury Becomes a Neighborhood

Once Golden Gate Park was underway, the Outside Lands Commission drew up plans for the private development of the Haight-Ashbury. Streets were named for Governor Henry **Haight,** City Supervisors Charles **Clayton,** Dr. Richard Beverly **Cole,** Monroe **Ashbury,** Charles **Stanyan,** and A.J. **Shrader.**

Henry Haight

Dr. Beverly Cole

The Lange House, Carl & Stanyan

The Land of the Fleas Becomes a Gentleman's Farm

Spanish colonists called it *La tierra de las pulgas*, the Land of the Fleas, and the native Ohlone avoided it, too. Early San Franciscans referred to the stretch of dunes to the City's west as "The Outside Lands." Despite the sand, wind, and other annoyances, in 1870, William Lange settled in the area that is now bordered by Cole, Stanyan, Carl, and Grattan Streets and established a successful dairy farm. The Lange family's Queen Anne house still stands at the **SE corner of Carl and Stanyan.**

The Popular Market Street Railway

In 1883, the Market Street Railway inaugurated its Haight Street line, bringing thousands of day-trippers to the park. Cafes, billiards halls, stables and bicycle shops sprang up along Haight and Stanyan Streets, as did other amusements, such as nickelodeons and saloons—**San Franciscans are never to be accused of not knowing how to have a good time!** The cable car turnaround at Haight and Stanyan was a bustling center of activity. Soon the wealthy began to build weekend homes in the Haight-Ashbury, so called because at that time Ashbury was considered the main intersection.

Crowds visit Golden Gate Park on the Market Street Railway, 1880s

The Chutes Amusement Park

The Chutes Amusement Park, 1895

In November, 1895, The Paul Boynton Chutes Amusement Park opened on Haight Street between Cole and Shrader. It included a Shoot-the-Chutes water slide, a zoo, an arcade, a beer garden, and a separate café for women and children. Vaudeville acts appeared on stage at The Chutes Theatre; the park was dismantled around 1900.

Midwinter International Exposition of 1894

From January 27th to July 5th, a world's fair was held in Golden Gate Park, attracting more visitors to the Haight. The first de Young Museum and the Japanese Tea Garden were originally built for this Midwinter Fair.

Midwinter Exposition 1894, Golden Gate Park

***1893** Lange's Dairy at Cole, Stanyan, Carl and Grattan streets*

***1906** The great San Francisco earthquake and fire.*

***1911-1916** Ishi, the last California Yahi Indian lives at UCSF*

1906 – 1960

Residences for the Wealthy Before and After the 1906 Earthquake

House on Ashbury Street

There was relatively little damage to the Haight-Ashbury in the Great Earthquake and Fire of 1906. The chert stone underlying the area is fairly stable, and the conflagration was stopped by a firebreak at Van Ness Avenue. Already an enclave of second homes for the wealthy, the Haight-Ashbury, and especially Ashbury Heights, became a desirable neighborhood for the permanent homes of successful San Franciscans such as Isaac and Mary Ann Magnin (I. Magnin Department Stores), **1231 Masonic Avenue.**

Park Branch Library

Since it opened in October, 1909, the neo-classical Haight-Ashbury Park Branch library has been a center of neighborhood activities. Generations of local children have spent countless hours enjoying books, the summer reading program and much more. The Haight-Ashbury Neighborhood Council, which was formed in 1960 to prevent the Panhandle's becoming an expressway, meets monthly in the library's community room.

Park Library, 1909

The 1930s and '40s

As early as 1890 large Victorian homes and Edwardian apartment buildings dotted the Haight. During the depression of the 1930s, many Victorian homes were divided into flats and rooms-to-let, which continued during WWII for workers who had arrived in San Francisco to build ships for the war.

WWII soldier on leave in the Haight

Ad for The Haight Grill, 1931 Haight & Ashbury

Haight Theater 1910

Haight Theater, 1941

The Haight Theater opened in 1910 on the northwest corner of **Haight and Cole**. It hosted vaudevillian acts and later became a movie palace. In 1964, the theater stopped showing movies and from 1966 to 1969 it became known as the Straight Theater; it was a local venue for the emerging acid rock scene. According to historian Reg E. Williams, "The Straight" opened in 1967 with appearances by **Quicksilver Messenger Service, Mount Rushmore, Salvation Army Banned, Mother Earth, Country Joe and the Fish, the Charlatans, the Grateful Dead, Big Brother and The Holding Company with Janis Joplin, Wildflower, Frumious Bandersnatch, Phoenix and others.** There was free music on Sundays, and every Monday was poetry night. The hippie community later held protests and a parade in attempts to prevent the landlord from tearing down the jewel of a building. Nevertheless, the theater was demolished in 1979.

Kezar Stadium & Pavilion

Opened in 1925, **Kezar Stadium** was the site for high school sporting events, professional sports, and acid rock concerts. Rebuilt below grade in the early 90s, the stadium continues to host a variety of sporting events and its jogging track is a place where neighbors often greet one another. **Kezar Pavilion** has been a famous Roller Derby venue since the '60s and more recently the home of the Pro-Am Summer Basketball League.

Kezar Stadium

1950s

Haight residents gather for a family portrait

In the '50s, the Haight-Ashbury was a neighborhood of long-time residents, workers who'd arrived during WWII, and new residents who'd found the Haight a welcoming place after "urban renewal" had forced thousands of African Americans out of their businesses and comfortable Victorian homes in the Western Addition and Fillmore districts. The affordability of apartments in The Haight brought in San Francisco State College (now University) students as well as beatniks relocating from the North Beach neighborhood, which was becoming pricier.

Straight Theater, handbill

Rusty Goldman collection

1914-1918 *World War I*

1929 *Stock Market crash and Great Depression*

1939-1945 *World War II*

1960s

What caused the Haight-Ashbury to become the center of a new social movement? Students and beatniks, followed by hip artists, musicians, and civil-rights activists, moved to the Haight-Ashbury for affordable digs in an accepting neighborhood and were known as **"hipsters"** and, derogatorily, as **"hippies."** LSD and other mind-expanding drugs (hallucinogens/psychedelics) began to be used by progressives around 1964. By 1965, the Haight-Ashbury proved an amenable place to begin the fusion of psychedelics and rock 'n' roll. Hip, psychedelic shops began opening on Haight, and by the summer of '67 (following plenty of publicity in the national media) anti-war activists and thousands of young people looking for alternatives to the conformity and materialism of post-WW II mainstream America flowed into the Haight.

A Social Revolution, a Sexual Revolution, the use of marijuana and other hallucinogenic drugs, and the development of psychedelic rock came together in a historic moment in the Haight in the late '60s.

Timothy Leary, Allen Ginsberg, Ken Kesey

CIA experiments with psychoactive drugs and the still-legal hallucinogen LSD sparked the interest of Harvard professor **Timothy Leary,** who was conducting The Harvard Psilocybin Project, studying the effects of mushrooms and psychotherapy. Beat poet **Allen Ginsberg** volunteered for the study, creating an association between the Beatniks and hallucinogens. Stanford graduate student and author **Ken Kesey** *(One Flew Over the Cuckoo's Nest)* had participated in studies at the Menlo Park VA hospital. On a trip to New York, after the publication of his book *Sometimes a Great Notion*, Kesey met Ginsberg, who introduced him to Leary. In 1964, Kesey led a group called **The Merry Pranksters** on a trip from La Honda, California to New York and back to California, in a **bus** with **"Further"** painted across the front. San Francisco was a home, of sorts, for Kesey. Ginsberg had an association with the Beatniks in the Haight, and both Ginsberg and Leary would participate in the 1967 **Human Be-In** in Golden Gate Park.

Lisa L...

Timothy Leary

SF Oracle

Allen Ginsberg

SF Ora...

Ken Kesey

The Psychedelic Era Begins

In January, 1966, brothers Ron and Jay Thelin opened the **Psychedelic Shop,** which became a center of activity, at **1535 Haight Street.** Ron, an army veteran, and Jay, his younger brother sold psychedelic paraphernalia, including the comics of R. Crumb, who lived in the neighborhood. With nearby **Mnasidika,** known as the first hip store, at **1510 Haight,** and other new shops such as **In Gear (1580 Haight),** which sold hip clothing, these businesses changed the face of the Haight-Ashbury in a lasting way. The owners of In Gear are still in the neighborhood; their Tribal Arts shop is located at **683 Haight Street.** As the psychedelic music scene began flourishing in the Haight, hundreds of young people were arriving daily, overwhelming the shops and services.

Outside The Psychedelic shop, Haight Street, 1966

SF Oracle

To complicate matters, the hip and psychedelic stores attracted a clientele that sometimes clashed with long-time residents and merchants, and the **Free Store**, started by the **Diggers,** was clearly at cross purposes with conventional commerce. Giving things away for free disrupted the established order. Places such as Roberts Hardware **(1629 Haight)** and Haight Street Shoe Repair **(1614 Haight),** both of which have been on Haight Street since the 1930s, and Mendels, which opened at Haight and Masonic in 1952 and moved to its current location at **1556 Haight** in 1968, struggled to balance their usual business with the influx of crowds and the vastly diverse clientele. The new businesses organized into the **Haight Independent Proprietors (HIP)** in an effort to give voice to the changes on Haight Street.

Herb Greene

Kids swarm to SF

1961
Vietnam War unofficially begins

1962
Marilyn Monroe, 36, dies of "acute barbiturate poisoning"

1963
President John F. Kennedy assassinated

Fillmore Auditorium, handbill, 1966

Wes Wilson, Joel Selvin

1960s

The Love Pageant Rally and the Human Be-In

Human Be-In, 1967

Lisa Law

On Thursday, October 6, 1966, the day LSD was declared illegal by the California legislature, the **Love Pageant Rally** was held in the Panhandle of Golden Gate Park. It was organized by *SF Oracle* founders Michael Bowen and Allen Cohen. Thousands of people, including Ken Kesey and the Merry Pranksters, gathered together, dropped acid, and heard the Grateful Dead and Janis Joplin play for free. The following January, on Saturday the 14th, between 20,000 and 30,000 people participated in the **Human Be-In**, also organized by Bowen, with assistance from Cohen. Timothy Leary encouraged those present to *"Turn on, tune in, drop out."* Beat poet Allen Ginsberg chanted mantras. The Hells Angels reunited children and adults who became separated in the crowd. The Grateful Dead, Jefferson Airplane, and Quicksilver Messenger Service played, and **Owsley Stanley** provided the acid. The Love Pageant Rally and the Human Be-in were bellwethers of the **Monterey Pop Festival** and the **Summer of Love**.

Owsley Stanley

Owsley Stanley

Though production of LSD (lysergic **acid** diethylamide) was legal in the U.S. until 1966, and possession until 1968, LSD wasn't always easy to find. First produced at the Sandoz labs in Switzerland in 1938, their LSD patent expired in 1963. In that year, former **UC Berkeley student Owsley Stanley** and his girlfriend chemist **Melissa Carghill** learned to make high-quality LSD, which they distributed in large quantities, often for free. He provided the LSD in the Haight-Ashbury, and also **"catered"** most of the psychedelic gatherings in and around San Francisco. In late 1967, Stanley was arrested for possession of 350,000 doses of LSD.

Monterey Pop Festival

The Monterey International Pop Music Festival (June 16-18, 1967) was a hugely influential kickoff to the Summer of Love. Peace, love, and orderliness abounded. Well-known groups such as The Mamas and the Papas, Simon and Garfunkle, and the San Francisco bands played along with artists who were about to become famous in the U.S., such as The Who and Ravi Shankar. For 25-year-old Otis Redding, who greeted the audience saying, ***"So, this is the love crowd,"*** Monterey was significant; he died six months later in a plane crash. The Monterey police seemed to develop a rapport with the concert-goers, there was a first-aid station, and the music was superbly performed. **The Monterey International Pop Music Festival** was hailed as a prototype for successful rock concerts and helped spawn the multi-billion dollar rock 'n' roll industry.

Tom Wilkes

Summer of Love 1967

Following the Love Pageant Rally in October 1966, the Human Be-In of January 1967, and the Monterey Pop Festival in June of that year, as many as **100,000 young people** came to the Haight-Ashbury. Media attention, from *The Oracle* underground newspaper, *the San Francisco Chronicle,* and a TV documentary, to a *Life* magazine article on LSD, fed the flames. The song **"San Francisco,"** written by the Mamas and the Papas' John Phillips and recorded by Scott MacKenzie, about **'flowers in your hair'** and **'gentle people there,'** contributed to the attraction of seekers to the Haight. The neighborhood quickly became overwhelmed.

Stanley Mouse, Rusty Goldman collection

1963
LSD first appears in sugar cubes on the streets of San Francisco

1964
President Lyndon Johnson wages war on North Vietnam

"You're either on the bus or off the bus."
– Ken Kesey

Lisa Law

1960s

The Oracle

The underground newspaper of the psychedelic movement was *The San Francisco Oracle*. Founded by Allen Cohen and Michael Bowen, *The Oracle* featured work by the beat writers **Lawrence Ferlinghetti, Gary Snyder, Lenore Kandel, Michael McClure,** and **Allen Ginsberg.** *The Oracle's* 12 issues, published from September 20, 1966 to February of 1968, were groundbreaking for their multicolored psychedelic art and subject matter: items of interest to the hippies in the Haight, including spirituality and philosophy.

SF Oracle

SF Oracle

Bill Graham

Wolfgang Grajonca, who would later change his name to Bill Graham, was among a group of German Jewish orphans who walked across France and later evacuated to the U.S. with the rise of the Nazis. In 1965, he dropped other career plans to become the manager of the San Francisco Mime Troupe, a group known for controversial street theater performances. On more than one occasion, the Mime Troupe's performances were fundraisers to cover their legal fees. Following ventures with Chet Helms and Family Dog, Graham set out on his own, producing many concerts to benefit the Haight-Ashbury Free Clinic, as well as other organizations. He worked with such groups as Country Joe and the Fish, Jefferson Airplane, and the Rolling Stones, and had an enduring and highly successful relationship with the Grateful Dead. Graham promoted many up-and-coming bands at **Winterland and the Fillmore** (later relocated and called the Fillmore West), in San Francisco, and the Fillmore East, in New York. The Fillmores closed in 1971. The venue at the original Fillmore building, at Fillmore and Geary, reopened in 1994. Bill Graham died in a helicopter accident in October, 1991.

Herb Greene

Bill Graham

"Who could have dreamed in 1965 that the alternative society would eventually multiply to such extraordinary proportions that it becomes our mainstream"

– Bill Graham

Hells Angels (& social club) House

The Hells Angels motorcycle club was at first antagonistic to anti-war protesters, but Ken Kesey and The Merry Pranksters and The Diggers won over the Angels. A 1967 New Year's party in the Golden Gate Park Panhandle with music by the Grateful Dead was a fundraiser for The Diggers organized by the Hells Angels. The Dead and the Hells Angels were neighbors when the Dead had the house at **710 Ashbury Street,** and the Hells Angels were just across the street. (Most people remember the address of the Hells Angels house as **719 Ashbury**.)

Hells Angels

"What the Summer of Love did for me like it did for so many people was produce a major transformation in consciousness for helping others."

– Dr. David E. Smith

Haight-Ashbury Free Clinic

Among the throngs of people attracted to the Haight-Ashbury, there were those whose **psychedelic experiences had unwelcome side-effects.** The most tangible and lasting response to the many health issues among the seekers in the Haight came from Dr. David E. Smith. Then not yet 30 years old, Dr. Smith founded the Haight-Ashbury Free Clinic. The clinic provided medical services to those in need, and Dr. Smith became renowned for his research of psychoactive, as well as addictive, drugs. Today, the Haight-Ashbury Free Clinics continue to serve those needing medical care.

Dr. David Smith

1965
Bob Dylan is booed off the stage at the Newport Folk Festival for playing electric guitar

1965
184,300 U.S. troops in Vietnam.

Malcolm X assassinated

1966
Life Magazine publishes cover article on LSD

LIFE ©

1960s

The Diggers

In 1966, some of the members of the San Francisco Mime Troupe formed a group called The Diggers. Emmett Grogan, Peter Coyote, Peter Berg, and others created The Diggers in the Haight as a form of community activism. The group's name was taken from The Diggers of **mid-seventeenth-century England**, who promoted shared property. In the Haight-Ashbury, The Diggers opened Free Stores *(see map)*, where everything was free for the taking and where people often swapped goods; served free food in Golden Gate Park; and organized free concerts by the Grateful Dead, Jefferson Airplane, and Janis Joplin, among others. They also worked with the Reverend Leon Harris, Rector, and members of All Saints Episcopal Church to provide a haven for homeless youth in the Haight.

The church is not a private club but rather... [it is] dedicated to supplying food, clothing and comfort to those in need, and hippies need these things."

– Rev'd. Leon Harris

© Ted Streshinsky Corbis

Diggers, handing out free food, 1966

Reverend Leon Harris

All Saints Episcopal, 1350 Waller Street

HANC
The Haight-Ashbury Neighborhood Council

HANC has a history of getting things done. Imagine, instead of the Panhandle greenbelt, a six-lane highway. That was the plan proposed in 1959 by the State Highway Department and supported by the city government. Two hundred Haight-Ashbury residents led the struggle to defeat the plan. The attempt was successful; the Panhandle was saved. As a result, **HANC adopted its by-laws in the spring of 1960** and has continually fought in the interest of its resident members of the Haight.

Death of the Hippie

On October 6, 1967, The Diggers staged **Death of the Hippie**, a mock funeral that emphasized the detrimental effects of the sensationalization of the hippie counter-culture by mainstream media. The Flower Children had become the media phenomenon **"hippies,"** and the message of the **"funeral"** was that the scene in the **Haight-Ashbury** was over and that people should carry out the message of peace and love wherever they were and **not come to the Haight**.

© Corbis

Death of the Hippie

"My advice to people today is as follows: if you take the game of life seriously, if you take your nervous system seriously, if you take your sense organs seriously, if you take the energy process seriously, you must turn on, tune in, and drop out."

– Timothy Leary

1966
385,300 U.S. troops in Vietnam, mass draft protests begin in U.S.

1967
485,600 U.S. troops in Vietnam

Fillmore Auditorium, handbill

Rusty Goldman collection

1960s

The San Francisco Music Scene emerged in the early 1960s as many formerly folk and folk-rock bands began to experiment with LSD and developed a new kind of rock 'n' roll—psychedelic rock. In 1963, Chandler A. Laughlin, III opened a traditional folk music club in Virginia City, Nevada called the **Red Dog Saloon**, where, by 1965, new Bay Area bands went to play and Bill Ham was doing his first light shows. The house band was **The Charlatans.** Other bands that played The Red Dog were the **Jefferson Airplane** and **Big Brother and the Holding Company**. Also playing there were **Jerry Garcia** and his band, the **Warlocks** (later the **Grateful Dead).** They had been hanging out in East Palo Alto, jamming, doing some gigs, and experimenting with hallucinogenic drugs.

Back in San Francisco, some of the people from The Red Dog were furthering the psychedelic experience. Calling themselves **"The Family Dog,"** they put on a couple of shows at the Longshoremen's Hall in Fisherman's Wharf and in the Haight-Ashbury. On the weekend of January 21-23, 1966, the Longshoremen's Hall was the site of **The Trips Festival** (a creation of "Prankster" **Stewart Brand,** later publisher of the *Whole Earth Catalog*, and others), and the new rock scene flowered like never before. It was Saturday night that **Owsley Stanley's** LSD punch was served; the Grateful Dead and Big Brother and the Holding Company performed. For many people there it was the first time they'd understood the full extent of the acid rock psychedelic experience.

The Bands

Chet Helms & Janis Joplin

Herb Greene

Chet Helms

Herb Greene

Chet Helms

Chet Helms played a major role in the psychedelic music scene in San Francisco. In 1961, Chester Helms met a singer named Janis Joplin in Austin, Texas. That was the year before he arrived in San Francisco. In the Haight-Ashbury, Helms started organizing jam sessions in Rodney Albin's Victorian basement ballroom at **1090 Page Street.** In the mid 60s, after starting the jam sessions there, Helms began developing groups and promoting events for the Family Dog, including events at the Fillmore and the Avalon Ballroom. He hooked up Janis Joplin with Big Brother and the Holding Company, and he arranged for their momentous appearance at the 1967 Monterey Pop Festival. Chet Helms also promoted Bill Ham's light shows, which became a longtime staple of psychedelic events. Helms later became an art dealer, promoting only a few events after the early seventies. One was the 30th anniversary celebration of the Summer of Love, a free event in Golden Gate Park (1997). Chet Helms died in 2005.

The Charlatans

Herb Greene

The Charlatans

Here's how San Francisco-based band The Charlatans came to be considered the first psychedelic, San Francisco Sound band. In June of 1965, the first time they played at **The Red Dog Saloon**, they dropped acid before going on stage. George Hunter was on autoharp, Richard Olsen played bass, Mike Ferguson was the keyboardist, Mike Wilhelm played lead guitar, and Dan Hicks was the drummer (replacing original drummer Sam Linde, after a short run). Everybody did vocals. They became the house band at The Red Dog, wore clothing inspired by 19th-century Wild West and Victorian eras, as well as Edwardian-influenced outfits, and then brought their style back to San Francisco and to the Victorian and Edwardian surroundings of the **Haight-Ashbury**. The band's nineteenth-century clothes had a major influence on young people's sartorial style. The Charlatans' first San Francisco performance was in August, 1965. They parted ways in '68.

1968
Martin Luther King, Jr. assassinated

1968
Robert Kennedy assassinated, 536,000 U.S. troops in Vietnam

Family Dog 1966

SF Oracle

1960s

Joel Selvin Collection

The Grateful Dead

The Grateful Dead

Jerry Garcia was a San Francisco kid. The founder of the Warlocks, who later became The Grateful Dead, was born on August 1, 1942 in San Francisco and grew up in the Mission and Excelsior districts. After attending the San Francisco Art Institute and later receiving a general discharge from the army, Garcia moved to East Palo Alto. It was there that he met first Robert Hunter, then Ron "Pigpen" McKernan, later Phil Lesh, and finally Bob Weir. A combination of an interest in folk and bluegrass, and curiosity about LSD—(which Hunter had been given in a study at the VA hospital where Kesey had been a participant)—created a mixture that would result in The Grateful Dead band and a phenomenal subculture. In September of '66, the Grateful Dead moved in to **710 Ashbury**. It was a pretty idyllic set up. Poet **Michael McClure** was raising a family in the neighborhood. The owners of the groovy new shop **In Gear**, and their daughters, lived a couple of doors down. The Charlatans, Amplified Ohm, Janis Joplin, and the Airplane, were all neighbors in the Haight. The Grateful Dead lived and jammed at **710 Ashbury** during the Indian Summer days of 1966. They were together until Garcia's death in 1995. Jerry Garcia's legacy continues, in music and in lifestyles that reflect Garcia's "think for yourself" philosophy.

The Great Society

Joel Selvin Collection

The Great Society

In August, 1965, Jerry Slick, a filmmaker, and his brother Darby, along with Jerry's wife, Grace, and friends David Miner, Bard DuPont and Peter Vandegilder formed the Great Society band. They played the Matrix and jammed at **1090 Page.** Of course, Grace Slick later became famous when she joined Jefferson Airplane upon the departure of Signe Anderson. Once Grace left, the Great Society folded in 1966.

Quicksilver Messenger Service

The band Quicksilver Messenger Service was made up of guitarists Jim Murray and John Cipollina, and Greg Elmore, David Freiberg (vocals), and Gary Duncan. Another friend, Dino Valente, was unfortunately incarcerated for possession when the band formed. He did, however, sing with them after a while. Dino's anthem *"Get Together"* is one of the most memorable songs from the Peace Movement. Valente's son and grandson continue his legacy and they can often be heard at Bay Area gatherings singing Dino's anthem, with the crowd joining in on the refrain that ends, ***"...and love one another right now."***

Quicksilver Messenger Service

Joel Selvin Collection

The Jefferson Airplane 1966

Barry Olivier

The Jefferson Airplane

Inspired by The Beatles and The Byrds, Marty Balin wanted to start a band. He and Matthew Katz started out doing folk and quickly switched to rock, forming The Jefferson Airplane, with Skip Spence on drums, Bob Harvey on bass, and Signe Anderson—a name in the San Francisco folk world as well as a denizen of the psychedelic community—doing vocals. Airplane was the house band at the Matrix, on Fillmore, owned by Balin and Katz.

Joel Selvin Collection

Jefferson Airplane (ca 1968)

Rusty Goldman collection

1969
500,000 people attend "Woodstock – An Aquarian Exposition: 3 Days of Peace & Music" (and rain)

1960s

Richard J. Hundgen Collection

Janis Joplin, Big Brother and the Holding Company

Among musicians in San Francisco in the early '60s, a girl from Port Arthur, Texas called Janis Joplin stood out. She'd arrived in San Francisco in 1963, living in North Beach and then the Haight, where she lived at **122 Lyon Street.** She began to be known for her bluesy style, and she recorded with Airplane guitarist Jorma Kaukonen in 1964. In '65, Joplin returned to Port Arthur to recover from heavy drug and alcohol use. In '66, Chet Helms got her to return to San Francisco and, later, join up with Big Brother and the Holding Company, a band founded by Peter Albin (Rodney's younger brother) and whom Helms was promoting. Janis and the band practiced at the Albin House, **1090 Page Street**, where other psychedelic bands also held jam sessions in the basement ballroom. Janis Joplin first performed with Big Brother at the Avalon Ballroom, on Sutter Street, in '66. Later that year, they had gigs as far away as Chicago, and they moved into a house in Marin with the Grateful Dead. By March, 1967, Janis was living at **635 Ashbury Street**, half a block from Haight. She roomed with her friend Linda Gravenites, who designed and created Janis' fantastic costumes. It was also in '67 that Janis and Country Joe McDonald had a romance. They lived together in the Haight for a spell, but the relationship was short-lived. In the summer of 1967, Janis and Big Brother made a huge impression on crowds (and promoters) at the Monterey Pop Festival. Big Brother and the Holding Company and Janis Joplin toured nationally in 1968, at one point performing with Jimi Hendrix, and had a gold album "Cheap Thrills," which included the hit single "Piece of my Heart." The cover for Cheap Thrills was designed by illustrator Robert "R." Crumb, who lived in the Haight at **1555 Oak Street**. Janis left the band at the end of 1968— she died of a heroin overdose in Los Angeles in October of 1970. Her ashes were scattered in the Pacific Ocean, off Stinson Beach.

Lisa Law

Janis Joplin, Big Brother & The Holding Company, left to right, back row: Sam Andrew, James Gurley, Peter Albin, Dave Getz, Janis Joplin

Herb Greene

"Oh Lord, won't you buy me a Mercedes Benz"

– Janis Joplin

Joel Selvin Collection

Blue Cheer, an American psychedelic blues-rock band performed in the late 1960s and early 1970s

1968
Demonstrations against the Vietnam War on college campuses

1960s

Jimi Hendrix

Jimi Hendrix concert at the Panhandle, 1967

With the help of British agent Chas Chandler, Jimi Hendrix hooked up with Noel Redding and Mitch Mitchell, bass and drums respectively, to form The Jimi Hendrix Experience. Hendrix's talent and charisma, and the musical expertise of these three musicians, made them a well-respected group. The Jimi Hendrix Experience played London and Stockholm (dedicating songs to Vietnam draft dodgers in Sweden) and gained international fame, but it wasn't until the Monterey International Pop Festival in June of 1967 that the band became known in the U.S. They played often in the Haight.

Electric Church of Jimi Hendrix

Country Joe & The Fish

"Country Joe" McDonald and Barry "The Fish" Melton started out as a protest band in 1965. Adding musicians as they went along, Country Joe and the Fish performed regularly at The Fillmore and the Avalon Ballroom and at anti-Vietnam War protest events. The band also performed at the historic 1967 Monterey Pop Festival. Like many other groups, Country Joe and the Fish split up in 1968. They had played their "I-Feel-Like-I'm-Fixin'-to-Die Rag" from the beginning, and that became their best-known song after McDonald's solo performance at Woodstock, in 1969.

Joel Selvin Collection
Country Joe & The Fish

Handbill—Rusty Goldman collection

1968 and the Aftermath

After the **Summer of Love,** those who remained in the Haight-Ashbury witnessed a harrowing scene. The media circus that focused on the Haight attracted self-serving types who took advantage of the situation in order to turn a profit. Dangerous drugs such as STP and THC were introduced into the LSD being distributed in the Haight. Rumors spread that the **CIA** was treating the Haight as a lab for drug experiments. There was an escalation of violence as heroin dealers moved in. City Hall turned Haight into a one-way street, and several of the shops were boarded up. Many of the people who came to Haight Street were shooting heroin and dealing hard drugs. The area around Haight and Ashbury came to resemble a militarized zone. Many Flower Children left the neighborhood, repairing to communes in the countryside. As the **1970s** began, the fallout from the Summer of Love was a harsh reality in the Haight-Ashbury. Vestiges of that time, iron-barred houses and storefronts, can still be seen today.

Handbill—Rusty Goldman collection

Lisa Law
Bring the troops home...

1968
Clashes between war protesters and police at the Chicago Democratic Convention

1969
250,000 people protest Vietnam war in Washington, D.C.

1970s

One outcome of the 1960s was that people began to feel more free to be themselves. With the 1969 Stonewall uprising, in Manhattan, The Gay Rights movement gained momentum. Second-wave feminism brought attention to Equal Rights for Women. Politically and personally, there were radical changes going on. As always, San Francisco proved to be a great place to be oneself, and the **Haight-Ashbury** reemerged as a counterculture haven. The I-Beam, located upstairs at **1748 Haight,** in the former Park Masonic Hall, was a "gay dance club" featuring the popular Sunday night "Tea Dance." Among the acts that played the club, which was open until 1994, were The Cure, Duran Duran, The Bangles, and Screamin' Jay Hawkins. Trax, 1437 Haight, a neighborhood bar, continues to be one of the city's best-loved gay spots.

Back-to-the-Land Movement

In the late 1960s and early '70s, so many people moved from urban to rural environments that a Back-to-the-Land movement was noted, even in census data. Many Flower Children left the Haight-Ashbury still seeking ways to change mainstream capitalism, politics, involvement in the war in Vietnam, and the destruction of the environment. Realizing that it's easier to change yourself than to change society as a whole, people became involved in self-realization movements, such as EST and the Jesus movement, and many were drawn to Buddhism. Some relocated to communes in the north—in Marin, Sonoma, and Mendocino counties—and beyond, where they shared domestic and social activities, and resources. With the help of Stewart Brand's *Whole Earth Catalog* and *Mother Earth News*, they also revitalized the **organic farming and environmental movements**, which continue to flourish today.

SF Oracle

Back to the Land, 1970

Punk Rock

In the Punk Rock scene of the 1970s, Haight Street was once again a counterculture hot spot. San Francisco was home to celebrated bands such as Mutants, the Dead Kennedys, and Flipper, who lived at **879 Haight Street.** The Sex Pistols' last performance was at Winterland on January 17, 1978, after which Sid Vicious took a non-fatal overdose at **32 Delmar Street.** He died in 1979.

Sid Vicious

"You can't arrest me, I'm a rockstar"
– Sid Vicious

Murals

Look for the many murals that have been painted in the Haight-Ashbury for decades. On the corner of Haight and Shrader are several graffiti-like murals, one depicting **Jimi**, **Janis**, and **Jerry**. The 1975 mural next to the Park Library is called **"Come Together."** On the west side of Cole St., near Haight, is the landmark Evolution Rainbow Mural, painted by **Yana Zegri** in 1969 and recreated by the artist in 2006. There is always a lively spray-painted mural across the street. As you walk east on Haight, turn around before you get to Masonic and admire the much-bigger-than-life-sized **Jimi Hendrix** painted on a wall above the north side of the street. The side of the building on the southwest corner of Masonic Avenue and Haight Street is most often used for ads painted by cutting-edge outdoor artists. Outside the bodega at the southwest corner of Haight and Central there's a mural that has sometimes been altered but usually depicts **Bob Marley** with a quote from him about valuing people over material things. The murals outside Hamilton Methodist Church depict scenes from the '60s. Indoor murals can be seen at **1530, 1538,** and **1727 Haight St**.

Jimi, Janis, and Jerry Mural at corner of Haight & Shrader

Mural on Waller Street at Hamilton Methodist Church

Mural at Haight & Cole

Mary Orr

"Unity in the Community" mural expressing racial and political solidarity in the Haight-Ashbury neighborhood. In the 1970s the mural was on the Black-owned Uganda Liquors at the corner of Haight and Masonic—now Positively Haight Street.

1970
The first Earth Day

1970
Native Americans land on Alcatraz Island and claim it as "Indian Land"

1973
Vietnam War ends; over 150,000 U.S. soldiers die in the 1957-1973 conflict

1974
Patty Hearst kidnapped; hides in Haight-Ashbury
Elvis Presley dies

1980s – Today

Dismantling of Social Programs

Down and out 1980s

In the 1980s, Ronald Reagan's Omnibus Budget Reconciliation Act (OBRA) cut federal funding to programs to assist the poor. Social programs that had been established by President Franklin Roosevelt's New Deal and President Lyndon Johnson's Great Society—though Johnson had made serious errors in Vietnam, he was effective in establishing social programs—suffered major setbacks. Many public institutions for people with psychological problems were shut down. This was a major cause of the chronic homelessness we know today. During the 1980s, the Haight-Ashbury saw an influx of underserved homeless people who had untreated psychological and addiction problems.

Food Not Bombs

Food not Bombs was founded in Cambridge, Massachusetts in the early 1980s, serving free meals in protest against money spent on war. In 1988, a second chapter of Food Not Bombs was formed in San Francisco. Volunteers began serving free food at the Haight Street entrance to Golden Gate Park as a protest against the City's anti-homeless policies. On August 15 nine volunteers were arrested. Free meals and over 1000 arrests continued into the 1990s. Currently, the San Francisco Food Not Bombs group serves meals at U.N. Plaza, in the Golden Gate Park Panhandle, and in the Mission neighborhood.

Food Not bombs, Buena Vista Park

Haight-Ashbury Food Program

From 1983 to 2008, the Haight-Ashbury Food Program provided hot meals four days a week to feed the hungry. Many Haight-Ashbury residents were among the volunteers, and lots of children growing up in the neighborhood share the memory of offering table service as among their family's favorite Thanksgiving traditions. In 2008, the Community Kitchen was replaced by the **Pantry Program**. Every Saturday, patrons come to the pantry, located on Waller near Belvedere, and choose foods that best fit their and their family's needs.

Red Vic Movie House

The Haight-Ashbury's movie house is the worker-owned-and-operated Red Vic. The collective began in 1980 and is now located at 1727 Haight Street. Audiences sit on sofas, or regular theatre seating, and can munch on organic popcorn, with or without a topping of brewer's yeast. The Red Vic shows current releases, premiers of indie movies, and classic cult films. A regular favorite is **"The Hippie Temptation,"** a made-for-TV film produced in August, 1967 by CBS and featuring then 44-year-old television journalist Harry Reasoner interviewing 25-year-old Jerry Garcia. The piece offers a look at the hippies, LSD, and psychedelic rock from the point of view of the cultural establishment. The film is said to have played a major role in piquing young people's curiosity about the Haight-Ashbury and the Summer of Love.

The people who started The Red Vic Movie House

Amoeba Music

A former bowling alley full of an enormous collection of music—rock, indie, jazz, folk, grunge, punk, standards, you name it, including films. Amoeba records has locations in Berkeley, someplace called "Holly-wood," and right on Haight Street, where the famous Rock-n-Bowl used to be.

1978: Homecoming & The First Annual Haight Street Fair

After a decade of hard times, Haight Street was to reemerge in a surprising way in 1978. Paul "Pablo" Heising had come to San Francisco with the Flower Children. In 1970 he had helped Harvey Milk with the Castro Street Fair and decided to try a Haight Street Fair in 1978. No one knew what would happen. There had been some renewal and gentrification in the neighborhood, but was it enough so that anyone wanted to attend? Artist David Wills created an enticing poster for the fair, and word got around town and spread among the Back-to-the-Land community. On April 30, 1978, Haight Street was the scene of an enormous **homecoming**. People who hadn't seen each other since '67 or '68 were reunited. "We met up with people whom we weren't sure had survived. It was beautiful!" said one man. The street and sidewalks were flowing with people, and there was an impromptu reunion of Flower Children at an after-party at the Shady Grove, at **1538 Haight**.

David Wills

First Haight Street Fair poster

The annual **Haight Street Fair**, which now takes place on the second Sunday in June, is a major event on San Francisco's calendar.

1980	***1991***	***2001***	***2003***	***2008***
John Lennon assassinated	*First Gulf War – Operation Desert Storm. Collapse of Soviet Union*	*September 11, al-Queda attacks on New York and Washington, U.S. invades Afghanistan*	*U.S. invades Iraq – here we go again*	*Barack Obama elected president*

FAMOUS HISTORICAL PEOPLE OF THE HAIGHT

Eldridge Cleaver

Eldridge Cleaver

Eldridge Cleaver became a spokesperson for the Oakland-based Black Panther Party in 1966. In the late '60s, Cleaver was acting president of the **Black Panthers** while Huey Newton was in jail. Cleaver's 1970 autobiography, *Soul on Ice*, became a best-seller. Among the pilgrims who came to visit Cleaver in his apartment at **436 Belvedere**, in the Haight, was actor Marlon Brando. Eldridge Cleaver died in 1998.

"Did I kill anyone?"
– Charles Manson

Charles Manson

Charles Manson

Born in 1934, Charles Manson lived in the Haight in 1968, in a garage in the **600 block of Cole Street**. There, he attracted a group of young followers, mostly female – the "Manson Family" cult. In 1969 he led the "family" to Los Angeles, where they brutally murdered actress **Sharon Tate** and others. Manson is now serving a life sentence at Corcoran State prison in California.

Marliyn Monroe

Marilyn Monroe

A few years before the Hippies arrived, Marilyn Monroe was often in the neighborhood at a friend's apartment at Casa Madrona, 116 Frederick Street. The sex-symbol actress stayed in the top-floor apartment to recover after completing her final film, *"The Misfits."*

Rudolph Nuryev & Margot Fonteyn

Rudolph Nuryev & Margot Fonteyn

The '60s in the Haight-Ashbury attracted even the glitterati. **Fonteyn**, considered the greatest prima ballerina of her time and **Nureyev**, whose dancing was so thrilling that he led male dancers into the spotlight, shared the stage and an intense friendship. In July of 1967, they shared the experience of being arrested together when anti-drug police raided the Haight-Ashbury party they'd been attending. The party was at **42 Belvedere Street**, and, according to reports, the two insisted on being busted along with their young hosts.

Peter Coyote

Peter Coyote

Peter was one of the founders of the **San Francisco Mime Troupe** and the **Diggers**, the improv group that provided free food, clothes, and medical attention to young people during the Summer of Love. He earned his master's degree in Creative Writing at San Francisco State and was an active member of West Coast communes. He's a playwright, a director, an actor and narrator, and an author. Rachmil Pinchus Ben Mosha Cohon, a.k.a. Peter Coyote, of Englewood, New Jersey, was a leading personality in the Haight during the Hippie Movement and now lives just to the north of San Francisco, in Marin County.

Lenore Kandel

Lenore Kandel

Beat Poet whose ***The Love Book***, published in 1966, was banned as pornographic and was the subject of a long-running obscenity trial whose appeal went to the California Supreme Court.

R. Crumb

R Crumb

"Keep on Truckin," "Fritz the Cat," "Mr. Natural," and now *"The Book of Genesis."* R. Crumb is the reigning king of underground comix. Crumb is originally from Pennsylvania, but he left his unhappy home there in the 1960s. First, he went to Cleveland, where he designed for the American Greetings card company while publishing in underground newspapers. In '67 he made his way to the Haight. Now living in France, Crumb was a founder of the underground comix movement, and first published **Zap Comix** in 1968.

"The only burning passion I'm sure I have, is the passion for sex"
– R. Crumb

Harry Bridges

Harry Bridges

Australian-American labor leader Harry Bridges lived at **1541 Shrader**. He was born July 28, 1901 and died in San Francisco on March 30, 1990. Bridges joined the International Longshoremens' Association local in San Francisco in 1924, participated in a Labor Day Parade, and was blacklisted for several years. He led the Albion Hall Group in a successful 5-day strike in 1933, and was chairman of the strike committee for the May 1934 **West Coast Longshoremen's Strike**, and the 4-day general strike in July of that year. Bridges was elected president of the ILA San Francisco local in 1935 and president of the ILA Pacific Coast District the following year.

"That's what a tribe is: people that are taking care of each other for real. Who care about each other. Who are mutually responsible for each other. Lovingly, Willingly."
– Lenore Kandel

PEOPLE OF THE HAIGHT TODAY

As you walk along **Haight Street**, you'll see high school students on lunch break, visitors from around the globe, homeless people, bike messengers, musicians—and you may catch a glimpse of a few of today's prominent Haight-Ashbury neighbors.

Stannous Flouride

Stan Flouride

Artist and history freak who has lived and worked in the Haight since the early 1980s. He has been been leading the **"Haight Ashbury Flower Power Walking Tour"** and randomly sharing his extensive knowledge of the neighborhood he has loved for many years.

Christin Evans and Praveen Madan

Haight-Ashburians and owners of **The Booksmith** independent book store.

The Booksmith, 1644 Haight St

Gavin Newsom

Fourth generation San Franciscan, youngest elected Mayor of San Francisco, from 2003 to 2011. He is known for the **Care not Cash** program to address homelessness, for authorizing **same-sex marriage** licenses, and for San Francisco's official support of the Kyoto Protocol (aimed at fighting global warming).

Pam & Bruce Brennan

The Brennans

Siblings Pam and Bruce Brennan, here in the '60s and still here today, are curators of the **Psychedelic History Museum** resident in their Victorian home turned B&B. Bruce, prior host of the TV cooking show *The Hippy Gourmet*, and Pam, preserve the Haight's colorful past by offering the **'Haight Ashbury Flower Power Walking Tour"** four times weekly, operate **The Herb'n Inn** (since 1988).

Dr. David E. Smith

Physician who came to the Haight in the 1960s, founded the Haight-Ashbury Free Clinic, and is a renowned expert on physchoactive drugs.

David Wills

David Wills

Artist, creator of the first Haight Street Fair poster (1978), blogger.

Diamond Dave Whitaker

Poet, activist, North Beach beatnik who moved to the Haight-Ashbury in the '60s, successful host of poetry readings

Craig Newmark

Founder of the website **Craigslist**, supporter of the cause of keeping the Internet free. See Map.

Laura Fraser

Travel writer and author of *An Italian Affair* and *All over the Map.*

Greg Gaar

Greg Gaar

Native San Franciscan who's been around the Haight for a long time. photographer, historian, native plants specialist, and champion of the Haight-Ashbury Recycling Center.

James Preston

James Preston, world renowned tie-dye artist, has been creating his works and operating the store **Positively Haight Street** for over 18 years. His tens of thousands of tie-dyes appear on clothing, tapestries and an album cover for The Grateful Dead. Visit the store for a chance to buy a tie-dye made by the artist directly connected to the history and music of the Haight.

The Red Victorian

Sami Sunchild

The building at **1665 Haight Street** at Cole was built in 1904 and opened as the Jefferson Hotel. During the **Summer of Love**, it was the Jeffrey-Haight, where people slept on mattresses on the floor, six to twelve people in a room, for $15-$18 a night. In 1977, when the Haight-Ashbury began to rebound after the decline following the Summer of Love, **Dr. Sami Sunchild** took over the building. It operates today as **"Red Victorian Bed, Breakfast and Art**," featuring the owner's peace-themed artworks. Rooms are named Rainbow, Sunshine, Flower Child and Summer of Love. As a peace activist, Dr. Sunchild has established the **Peaceful World Foundation**. She says, *"At the Red Vic we demonstrate that cultural tourism can offer positive, educational experiences to travelers, and that it can be a sustainable business enterprise for individuals, families and even villages around the world."* Everyone is invited to participate in World Conversations at the Red Victorian over breakfast every Sunday morning at 9:00. The **Peace Cafe**, on the ground floor, offers evening events that include readings and live music. A stay at the Red Victorian, or even just stopping for a bite at the Peace Cafe, usually involves meaningful exchanges with interesting people from all over the world.

- Famous Stars
- Famous Residents
- *Historical Haight Site* *(no longer exists)*
- Retail
- Restaurant/Cafe
- Lodging
- Point of Interest
- Golden Gate Park Shuttle Route & Stops *(Weekends only)*
- Muni Bus Route
- Muni Metro Route *(dashed = underground)*
- Restroom/Toilet
- Parking
- Bicycle Rental
- ATM

Please note: *The Musicians, Stars and Famous People shown on this map no longer live in these locations. Please respect the privacy of the people who currently occupy these buildings today.*

The following is an incomplete sampling of places to shop and eat in the Haight. As you explore the neighborhood, you will find an extraordinary and unique collection of other shoe, smoke, gift and clothing shops, cafés, tattoo parlors and much more...

Shop the Haight

1 **Alpha market:** 960 Cole, local grocery, sandwiches

2 **American Apparel:** 1615 Haight, cool, edgy, simple clothes

3 **Amoeba Music:** 1855 Haight, vast selection of music & movies

4 **Booksmith:** 1644 Haight, the neighborhood's landmark bookstore – known for its award-winning author events program

5 **Cheap Thrills:** 1687 Haight, gag gifts

6 **Cal Surplus:** 1541 Haight, military, camping and traditional work gear

7 **Cole Hardware:** 956 Cole, if you can't find it here, it probably doesn't exist

8 **Cole Valley Antiques:** 90 Parnassus, small, but packed with the unusual

9 **Dollhouse Betty:** 1641 Haight, classic lingerie

10 **Earthsong:** 1701 Haight, unusual women's clothing and gifts

11 **Egg + Urban Mercantile:** 85 Carl, eclectic housewares

12 **Fluevog:** 1697 Haight, fashion forward shoes

13 **Fresh Organics:** 750 Stanyan, fresh, organic-only produce

14 **FTC Skateboarding:** 1632 Haight, skateboarding gear

15 **Genesis Imports:** 1573 Haight, spiritually oriented gifts

16 **Giant Robot:** 618 Shrader, if you have to ask...

17 **Goodwill:** 1700 Haight, second hand clothing

18 **Goorin Brothers:** 1446 Haight, millinary, great selection of hats

19 **Haight-Ashbury Music Center:** 1540 Haight, long-time purveyor of musical instruments and sheet music

20 **Haight Street Market:** 1530 Haight, where the locals shop to restock the pantry or get a snack to go

21 **Haight Street T-shirts:** 1500 Haight, stickers, patches, and other memorabilia

22 **Kidrobot:** 1512 Haight, pop culture toys

23 **Kids Only:** 1608 Haight, hip clothing and gifts for children

24 **La Rosa:** 1711 Haight, fine vintage wear

25 **Love of Ganesha:** 1310 Haight, clothing and gifts from Southeast Asia

26 **Mendels:** 1556 Haight, Far-Out-Fabrics, Art store and so much more!

27 **Neda's Gifts and Flowers:** 1681 Haight, vintage curiosities

28 **Pharmaca Integrative Pharmacy:** 925 Cole, holistic health products and remedies, full pharmacy

29 **Piedmont:** 1452 Haight, glam-rock duds, most made by the owner

30 **Pipe Dreams:** 1376 Haight, since 1978

31 **Positively Haight Street:** 1400 Haight, tie-dye clothing, crafts, gifts

32 **RCVA:** 1485 Haight, lifestyle clothing

33 **Recycled Records:** 1377 Haight, excellent selection of used records

34 **Roberts Hardware:** 1629 Haight, hardware since 1931

35 **The Red Victorian Peace Center Gift Shop:** 1665 Haight, peace-centered art by Sami Sunchild

36 **The Sword and Rose:** 85 Carl, astrologic, tarot, occult

37 **Villains Vault:** 1653 Haight, jeans and casual chic

38 **Wasteland:** 1660 Haight, vintage and hip clothing

39 **Whole Foods Market:** 690 Stanyan

Cafes/Restaurants

1 **Alembic:** 1725 Haight, outstanding bar; relaxed chic

2 **All You Knead:** 1466 Haight, local dining place; casual

3 **Bambino's Ristorante:** 945 Cole, family-style neighborhood pizza, casual Italian

4 **Ben & Jerry's:** 1480 Haight, scoop shop and treats

5 **Bia Restaurant and Wine Bar:** 1640 Haight, they use organic produce; casual chic

6 **Boulange de Cole Valley:** 1000 Cole, Parisian-style, people-watching café & bakery

7 **Blue Front:** 1430 Haight, falafel and hummus Mediterranean café

8 **Café Cole:** 609 Cole, juice bar, coffee, pastries

9 **Cha Cha Cha:** 1801 Haight, fun Cuban eatery; casual chic

10 **Citrus Club:** 1790 Haight, Pacific Rim, noodle-based dishes are a specialty; casual

11 **Club Deluxe:** 1511 Haight, bar which occasionally hosts live music & standup

12 **Coco Luxe:** 1673 Haight, exquisite chocolate and wine

13 **Coffee to the People:** 1206 Masonic, neighborhood coffee shop

14 **Cole Valley Café:** 701 Cole, coffee and sandwiches

15 **Eos Restaurant and Wine Bar:** 901 Cole, Asian-fusion, extensive wine list, home-made ice-cream

16 **Escape from New York:** 1737 Haight, open late, pizza by the slice

17 **Grandeho's Kamekyo:** 943 Cole, friendly neighborhood sushi bar, casual

18 **Hama-Ko Sushi:** 108B Carl, cozy, exotic traditional sushi, casual

19 **Hobson's Choice:** 1601 Haight, large selection of rums

20 **Kan Zaman:** 1793 Haight, hookah bar with Mediterranean small plates

21 **Kezar Pub:** 770 Stanyan, wings served at this sports bar

22 **Magnolia Gastropub and Brewery:** 1398 Haight, formerly the "Drogstore," during the Summer of Love; named after a '60s personality, Magnolia Thunderpussy; casual, open late

23 **Martin Macks:** 1568 Haight, Irish bar always has a sports game on

24 **McDonalds:** 730 Stanyan, standard American fast food

25 **New Ganges:** 775 Frederick, vegetarian and Indian cuisine

26 **Panini:** 1457 Haight, warm toasted sandwiches and café

27 **Peace Café/Red Victorian:** 1665 Haight, vegetarian, vegan, organic entrees, fair trade coffee, breakfast, lunch and dinner

28 **Pork Store Café:** 1451 Haight, a former butcher shop, casual, good for brunch

29 **People's Café:** 1419 Haight, juice bar and café

30 **Ploy II:** 1770 Haight, Thai overlooking the busy street below

31 **Reverie Café:** 848 Cole, favorite local coffee bar–sunny in the afternoon, casual

32 **Say Cheese:** 856 Cole, Cheese, wine, charcuterie and sandwiches

33 **Tully's Coffee:** 919 Cole, local espresso – sunny in the morning, casual

34 **Zam Zam:** 1633 Haight, (in)famous local bar

35 **Zazie:** 941 Cole, French-inspired Mediterranean menu, casual

36 **Zona Rosa:** 1797 Haight, Mexican Taqueria

URY

Legs: *1452 Haight—one of the most photographed signs in San Francisco!*

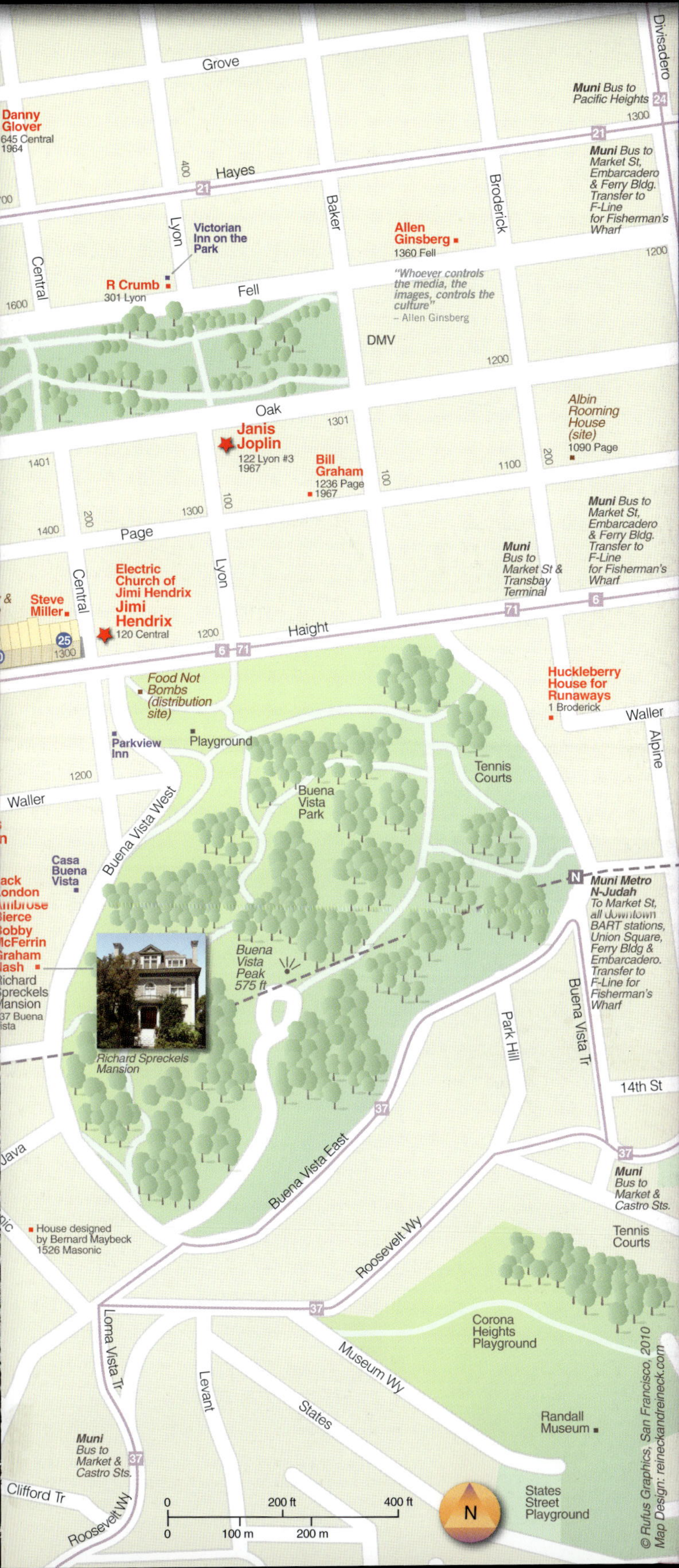

THINGS TO DO IN THE HAIGHT

The Haight-Ashbury Flower Power Tour
www.haightashbury-tour.com

San Francisco City Guides Tour
www.sfcityguides.org
Sundays

Flashback, by Foot! comedy walking tours
http://www.foottours.com/tours/flashback

Haunted Haight Walking Tour
(415) 863-1416
www.hauntedhaight-tours.com

Other Tours
www.sfhistory.org

Shop/Cafes/Restaurants
See Map and page16 for selected list of locations

Haight Street Fair
Second Sunday in June

See Where Famous People Formerly Lived
See Map for other locations

Grateful Dead
710 Ashbury

Hell's Angels
719 Ashbury

R. Crumb
301 Lyon

Janis Joplin
122 Lyon, 635 Ashbury and 1275 Waller

THINGS TO DO NEARBY

See Map

Golden Gate Park & Panhandle

Golden Gate Park, just west of the Haight-Ashbury, is full of things to see and do. A park-wide shuttle runs every 15 minutes on weekends and major holidays ($2/person). Some of the oldest trees in San Francisco are among the **Panhandle's** hundreds of tree varieties. The Panhandle Playground includes a climbing structure, basketball courts, and restrooms.

Children's Playground, Golden Gate Park

Children's Playground (Koret Children's Quarter)

The **oldest public playground** in the United States and the nearby **carrousel** opened at the same time, in 1888. The carrousel operates daily, 10 am. to 4:15 pm from Memorial Day through Labor Day, and Fridays, Saturdays & Sundays all year.

Hippie Hill

Across Sharon Meadow from the playground, where, midday on week-ends and often during the week, you're likely to hear a drum circle, attracting participants and dancers of all ages.

National AIDS Memorial Grove

Begun in 1991, the memorial has been dedicated as a space for remembrance, renewal, and hope.

Conservatory of Flowers

Conservatory of Flowers

Erected in 1878-9, this is the **oldest** wood and glass conservatory in North America. It's a city, state, and national historic landmark.

Japanese Tea Garden

Created for the Midwinter Fair of 1894, it is the **oldest public Japanese Tea Garden** in North America. Visitors can enjoy Buddhas, bridges, native Japanese plants and ponds, as well as a tea house and gift shop.

Museums

The **de Young Fine Arts Museum** houses American art from the 17th century through today, and art of the Americas, Africa, and the Pacific, in its world-renowned building designed by Herzog & de Meuron. Visit the spectacular viewing tower. The museum is closed on Mondays. The **Academy of Sciences** designed by Renzo Piano, features an aquarium, planetarium, rain forest and roof garden. The museum has regular hours every day.

Rental boats, Stow Lake

Stow Lake

Huntington Falls and the Chinese Pagoda are on the eastern side of Strawberry Hill, surrounded by Stow Lake. On the western end, there's a boa house with rowboats and paddle **boats for rent**, as well as a snack bar. In the parking and picnic area behind the boat house, visitors can **rent bikes** anc pedal-powered surreys.

Cole Valley

A few blocks south of Haight Street lies leafy Cole Valley. Quaint shops and restaurants line village-like Cole Street. The annual Cole Valley Street Fair is on a Sunda in late September.

The Randall Museum

Exhibits on local flora an fauna and some history—directed primarily at children—with live hawk and other wildlife to observe up close, a petting area with small farm animals, beautiful views and a picnic area. The Randall is open 10 am to 5 pm, Tuesday through Saturday; closed on major federal holi-days, admission is free. The Golden Gate Model Railroad Club's train layout is open Saturdays 10 am to 4 pm.

Buena Vista Park

The **oldest park in San Francisco**, rises about 569 ft. above sea level. I began as Hill Park, in 1867, and became Buer Vista in 1894. The park includes a redwood and live oak groves, and retaining walls made of former headstones from old San Francisco cemeteries. There's a dog run, and the playground is a favorite spot for neighborhood families with children. **A hike to the top of the hill is rewarded with stunning views**.